CHORDS & RHYTHM
NEXT LEVEL TECHNIQUES

THOMASINA WINSLOW

Thomasina Winslow

Copyright © 2021 Thomasina Winslow

All rights reserved.

ISBN: 978-0-578-26667-1

Thomasina Winslow

CONTENTS

	Acknowledgments	i
1	Section I: Put Some Pepper in Your Progressions	1
2	Section II: Capture Your Audience with Signatures	15
3	Picking and Strumming	16
4	Dynamics Matter	17
5	Let Your Fingers Do the Talking	18

Thomasina Winslow

ACKNOWLEDGMENTS

I would like to acknowledge my family and friends. To my brothers who are absolute princes in their lives. To my dear friend E.J. OakLore who has been a supportive force and who generously and selflessly has used his talents to help me make my dreams of authorship and artistry become a reality. And to my late but never forgotten parents Thomas Winslow and Edral DuBois Wynn Winslow who raised me to be confident through all situations and have taught me the art of determination. And finally, to my students who have been my teachers in many ways as I have developed my STEAM (Strength Through Expressive Arts Mentoring) lesson program and this book for their enjoyment and progression ever forward. I love you all enjoy!

Thomasina Winslow

Thomasina Winslow

Section I

Put Some Pepper in Your Progressions.

I want to be clear that this is *not* a lesson book. What I have put in this book for you, assumes some basic knowledge of the guitar. This surpasses a lesson book, and what I mean by that is that you will go beyond learning how to make chords and the ups and downs of strumming and rhythm patterns. What I want to demonstrate to you is the way that you can capture the attention of an audience by making those chords and rhythms capture their attention.

So, I will show you some ways to spice up the chords with a little extra pepper using creative strumming techniques. Strumming is great, and a creative strummer can play a song and the audience will know the song by the chord progression. If you stick to the chord progression you will be fine, but what if you played the signature patterns and progressions that the audience recognizes? They will love it!

I will demonstrate this with three chord progressions. For simplicity's sake let us do the

I – IV – V progression in the following keys.

The Key of E: E - A - B or B7

The Key of C: C – F - G

The Key of G: G – C – D

Believe it or not each one of the chords has a special kind of spice that you can add to it by adding or subtracting notes in the chords. Refer to the audio library CD to demonstrate each of the chords mentioned. It will become clearer when you listen to it. Let us begin with E major our I chord in the key of E major. Below is the full chord. I will assume knowledge of chord charts. Just in case though here is how.

index on the 1st fret of the 3rd (G) string

middle on the 2nd fret of the 5th (A) string

ring on the 2nd fret of the 4th (D) string.

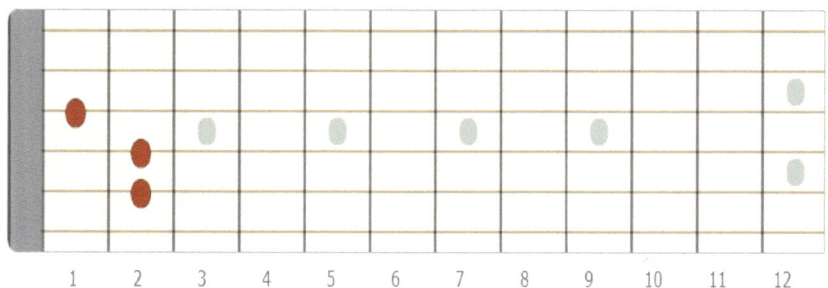

Ex. 1. The first bit of pepper is lifting and replacing the index finger. It looks like an E minor but played only in passing. See how that sounds.

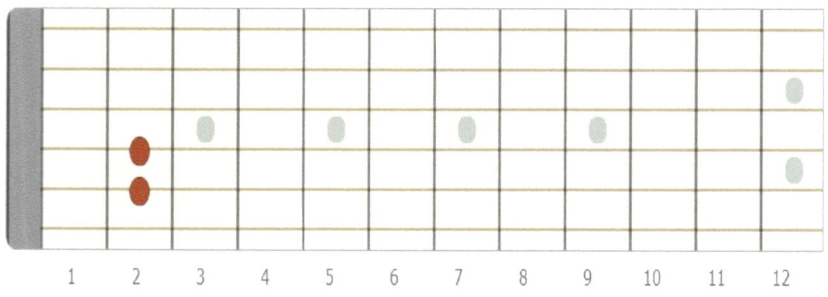

Ex. 2. Next is to do the same with the middle finger. See how it sounds

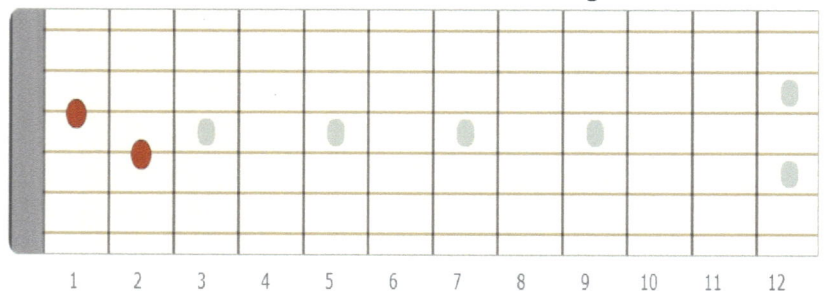

Ex. 3. Finally, do the same lifting the ring finger. See how that sounds.

Chords and Rhythm: Next Level Techniques

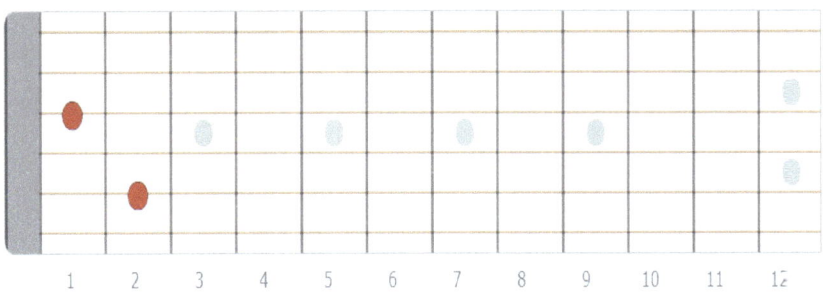

Now you have expanded the use of this chord and you can decide what sounds best to you or if you hear a song that you want to cover, and any of these are played you will recognize them right away. Your ear is going to be so sharp now! You will be hearing what you have played and relating it to what you hear others play.

This is a good start to also writing songs or instrumentals. You do not have to always relate the gestures that I demonstrate to you on cover songs, but you will begin to write your own songs and have an expandec musical vocabulary with chords.

Let's move on to the A chord which is the IV in the key of E major. Same thing applies here. You are playing passing tones and suspensions once again.

Here is the full chord. These are all first position chords by the way.

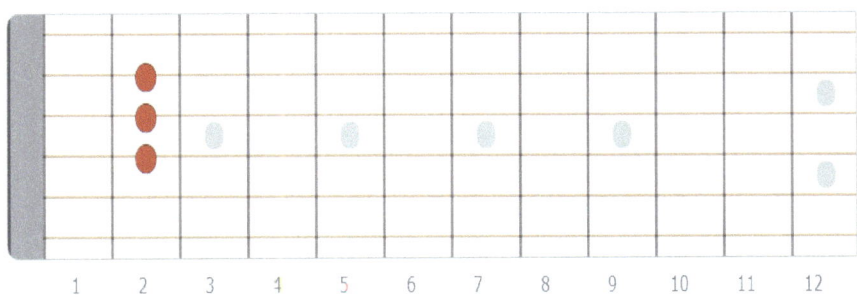

Ex. 4. Here is the A major chord lifting and lowereing the index finger.

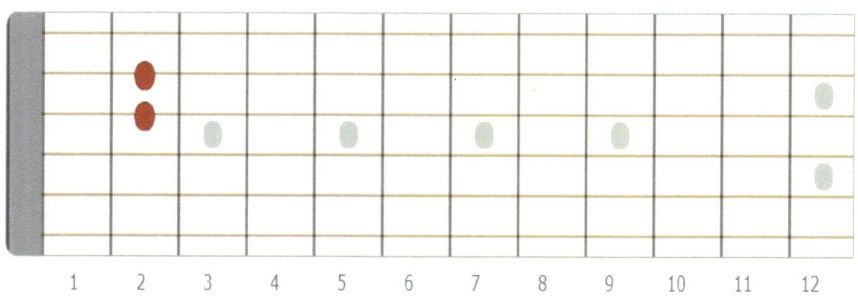

Ex. 5. Here is the same chord with using the middle finger the same way. It is an A7 chord played this way.

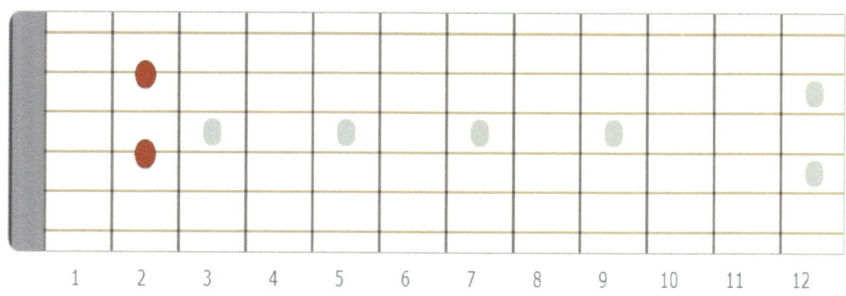

Ex. 6. And finally, the same chord using the ring finger to change the sound.

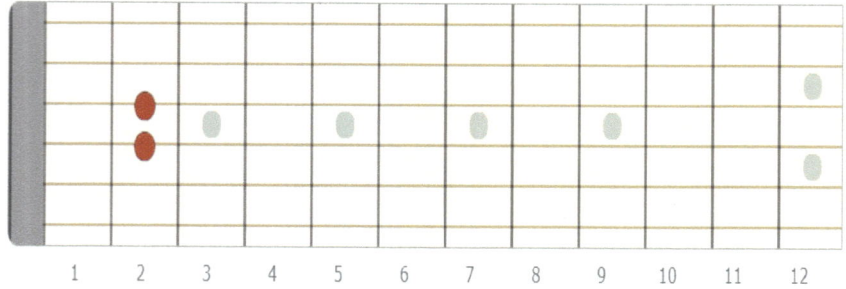

Take a listen to the audio and it will become even more clear.

We are on a roll so let us go to the V chord which is B7. This is the full chord.

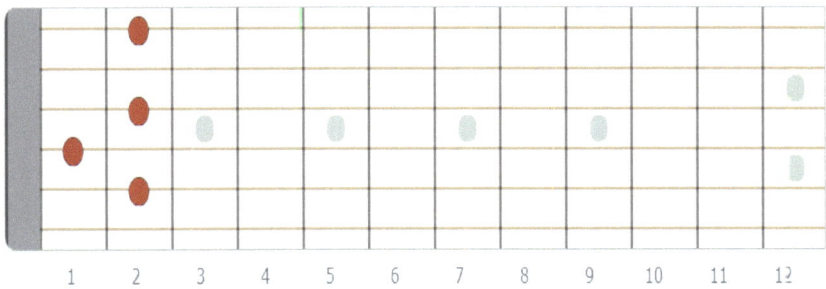

Ex.7. What we are going to do first with this chord is move it up a fret and back down to regular position. Here it is up a fret. Take a listen to the audio ideas for this.

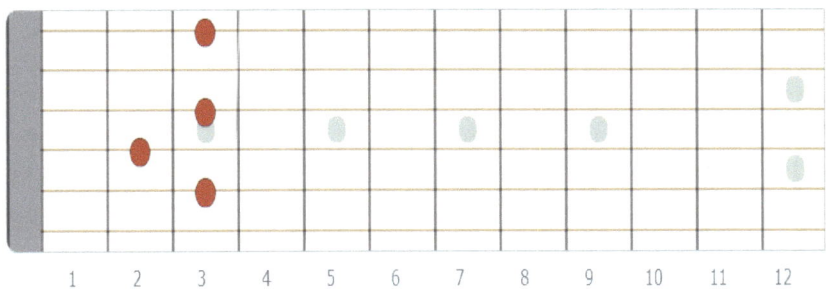

Ex. 8. Here is another great move. You can move your middle finger to the second fret of the 6th string which will give it an interesting sound. Take a listen to the audio for this I think you will find it interesting.

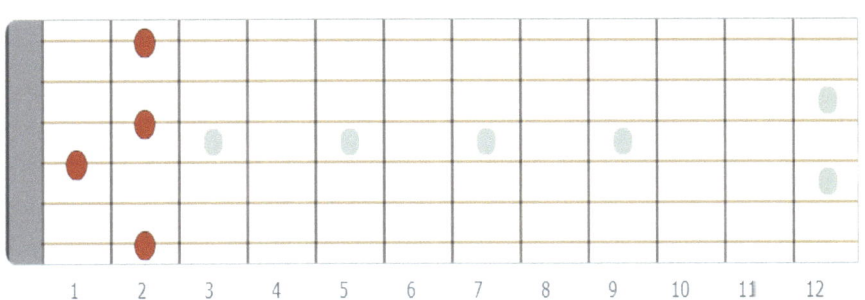

Ex. 9. You can do the usual lifting of fingers like we did for the E and the A and Ex.9 will expand on that.

I think you get the idea about that for this key. Let's continue with our keys and move on to the key of C. Same thing here with a few surprises that will sound great.

Here is the C chord.

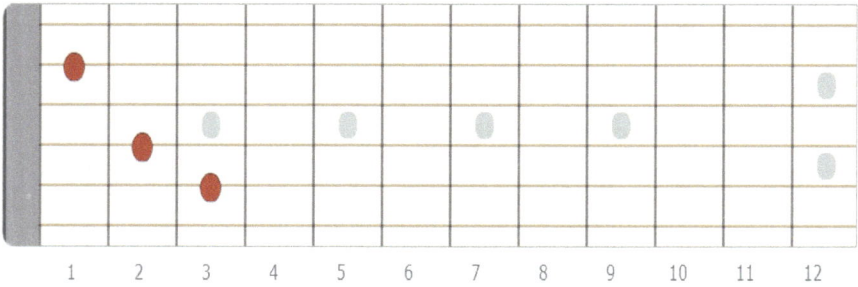

Ex. 10. Here is what is called C2 that is because the D note on the B string is added. This will sound familiar to you because there are a lot of songs in alternative rock that use this chord. Take a listen to this track on the audio file or CD.

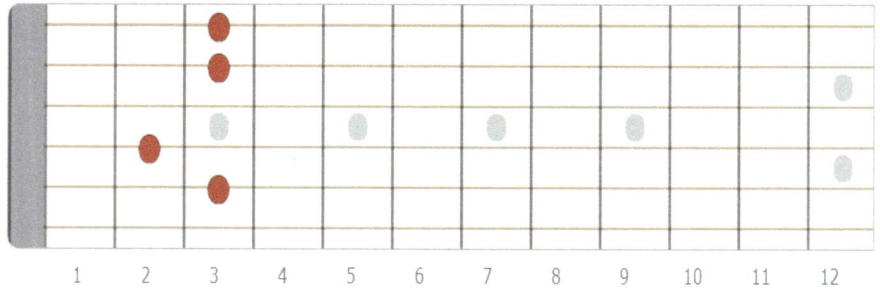

Ex. 11. Back to the regular first position C chord lifting the index finger. Play around this that and see how it sounds to you.

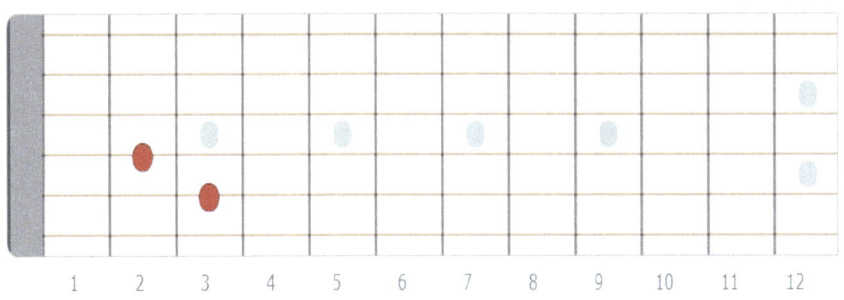

Ex. 12. For the sake of consistency here is the C chord lifting the middle finger.

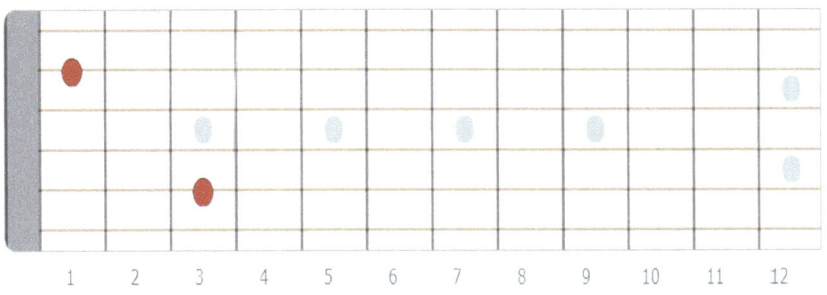

Ex.13. Here is the C chord lifting the ring finger.

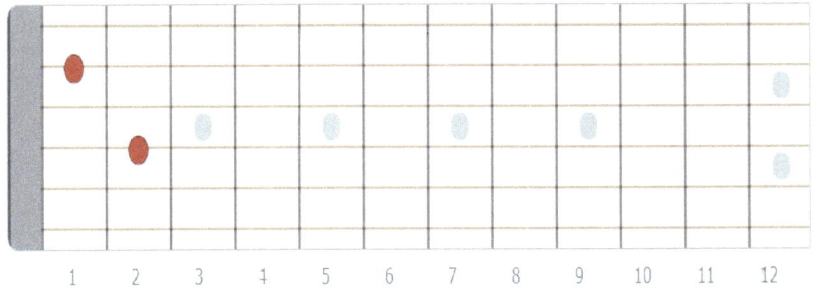

Before I go on to the other chords in this key, I want to explain further why this is important. It is good to know what you can do with the first position chords. Later you can find these chords along the neck using barre chords partial chords and even double stops. There is not enough room to put all these things in one book so there may need to be another volume, but you have plenty to do with this. If you get too bogged down, then you will not be able to hear anything. Your ears can shut off. Later, I will cover some ideas for how you can keep your ears fresh. Letting them rest is the first and best step.

Let's finish up with the first position chords.

The IV chord in the key of C is F. Here it is in first position.

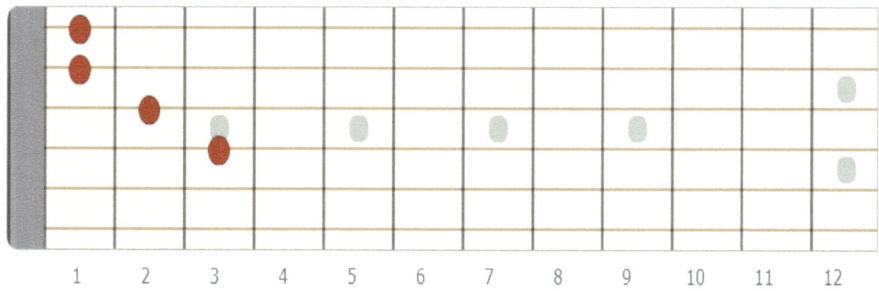

Ex. 14. If you want to add the bass note 'F' on the 6th string without playing a full barre chord, you can hook your thumb over the 1st fret of the E string. This is what that would look like.

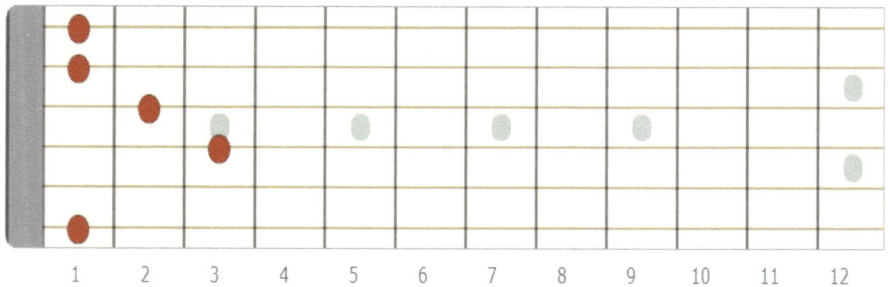

Ex. 15. If you are like me and most other guitarists, you loathe the F chord because of that hinge barre on the E and B strings. Here is an interesting sound you can play with. The F without that barre. It really is a sweet sound so noodle around with it.

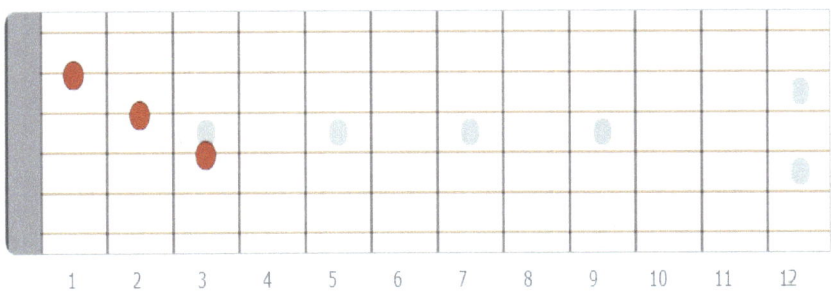

Ex. 16. I used the word noodle because despite what some may tell you "noodling" is the path to discovery for guitarists. Another reason for this is that it is a good way to warm up your hands. You never want to play not having warmed up. That does not mean that you must use scales for every warmup session but along with scales you really should try some other musical things like phrases or simply moving some chords around to also warm up your ears. What I am giving you here is direction for your noodling. I cannot wait to hear from you about what you have come up with. In keeping with our pattern here is the F chord lifting the index finger.

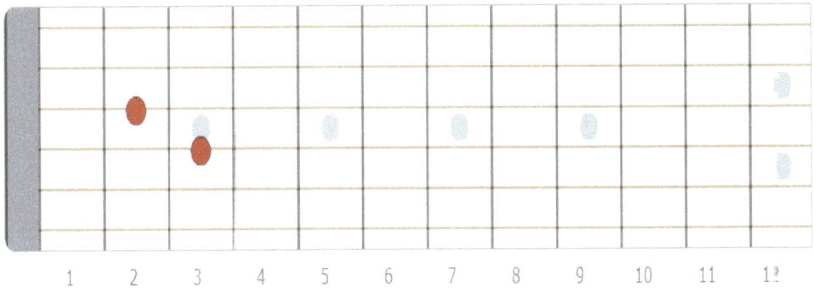

Ex.17. Lifting the middle.

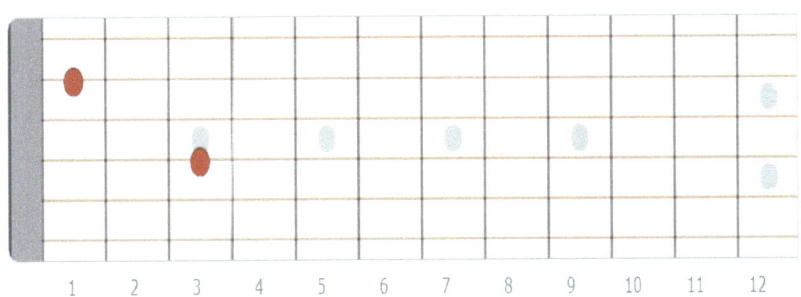

Ex. 18 *audio only*. Lifting the ring finger sounds weird but may be good as a passing tone. See what you think. Your decision may be different than mine.

Let us move on to the last two chords in this chapter starting with the V of C which is G.

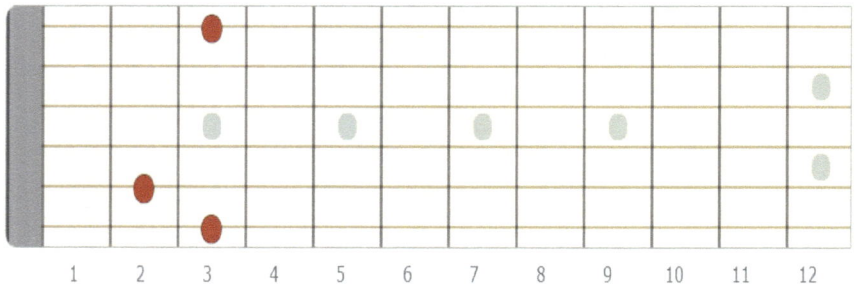

Ex. 19. The G chord has its own little rules and quirks so what we have done does not necessarily apply for G. Here is the G5 which looks like the C2 because of that 'D' note on the 2nd or B string. Again, a very popular and familiar chord as you will hear in the sound sample.

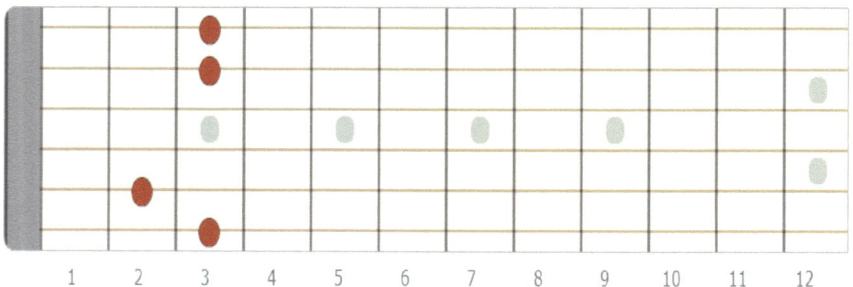

Ex. 20. This is a cool one. Basically what you are doing is moving your index and middle finger into a C chord while keeping your ring finger placed on the third fret G of the 6th string. You will hear this figure over again as you listen to music.

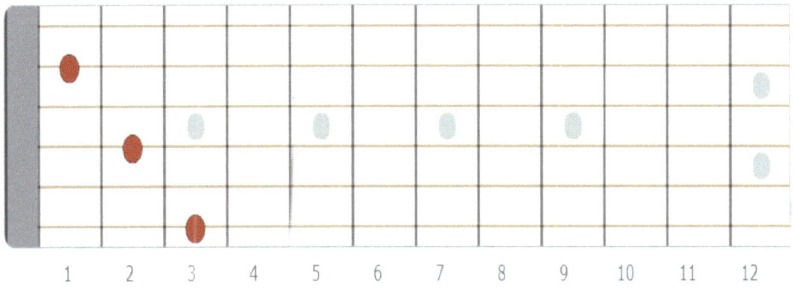

Ex. 21. This is the G7 chord. Needs no further explanation.

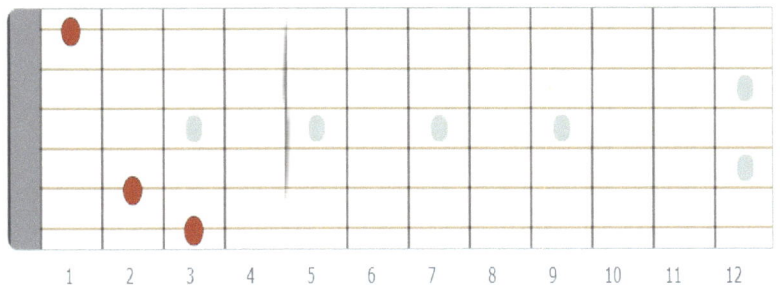

Ex. 22. The last one I will go over for G is the lifting of the index finger. Play around with that see how it sounds.

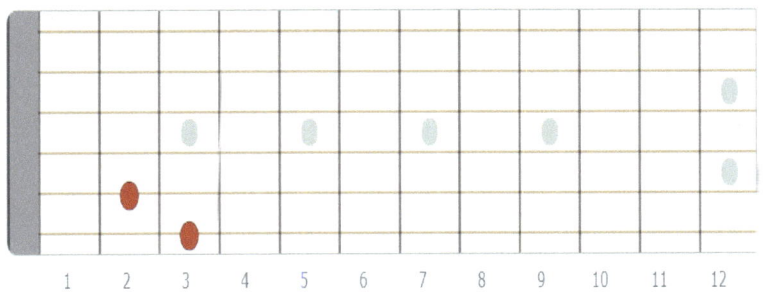

We have come to the last chord which is D. D has its own rules to so let's get to it. Here is regular D chord.

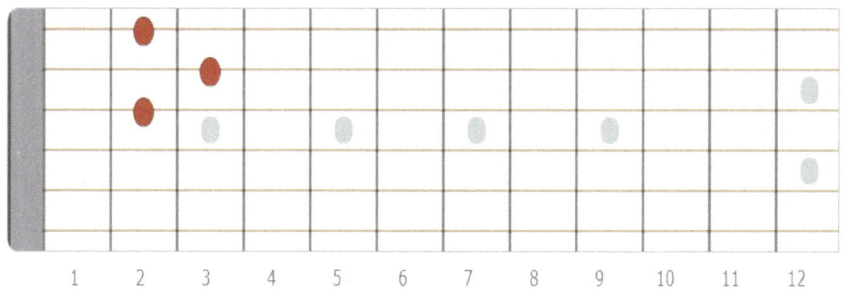

Ex. 23. There is a nice figure called the Dsus chord which means D suspended, and you will recognize it on the audio sample. This chord can make anything you play or write sound really pro.

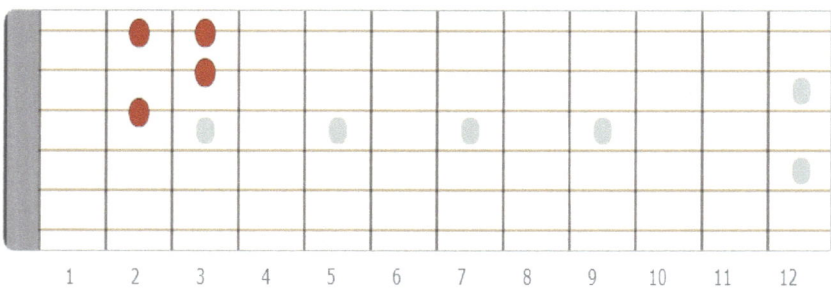

Ex. 24. D minus the index finger

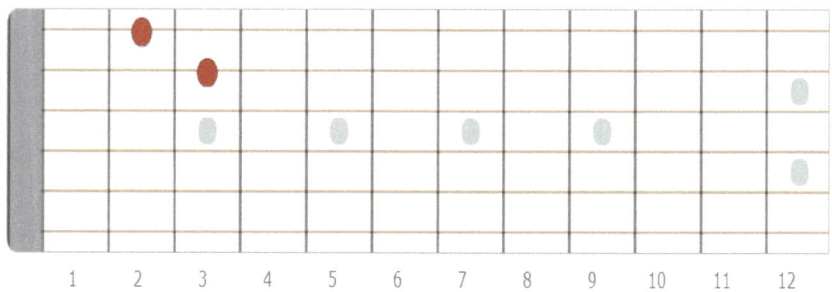

Ex. 25. D Minus the middle finger.

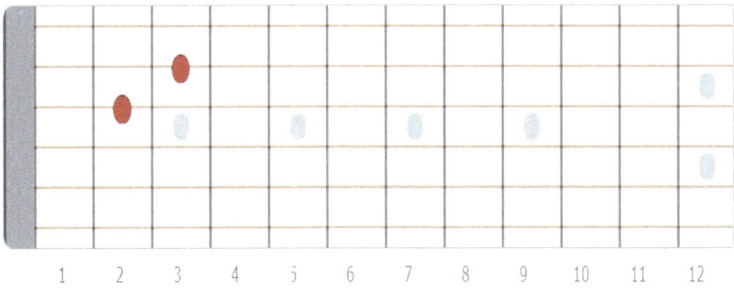

Ex. 26. Minus the ring finger.

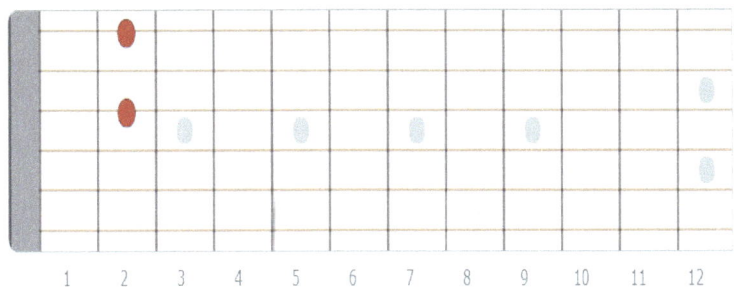

So, there you have it. There are at least four or five ways of peppering all your major chords from A to G. You can apply the same to your minor chords. In musical terms you are adding color to the chords and progressions. What is the point of this? First, this will help you boost the writing of your originals, and secondly perform your chosen covers to the highest level.

It is good to know the specific musical terms because you are not at the beginning, and this is not a lesson book but a book of techniques that will help you create and appear to perform effortlessly. But you and I know that this is not effortless. Your audience may not know the work that you have put in, but they will appreciate it and help make your gigs worthwhile.

Enjoy the work! Let me know how it goes when you hit the stage!

Section II

Capture Your Audience with Signatures.

The simplest way to describe signatures is that they are musical gestures or motifs that identify a song. It could be in the non-vocal instrumental music or a vocal singable signature for example the song "Sweet Caroline" by Neil Diamond. This is a song that reaches across many generations since its first release, and everybody knows the horn part and sings it... "Ba Ba Baa!" (*"Good times never felt so good... "etc.)*

The signatures are what makes songs recognizable as what they are. As a performer the ability to "signature" your covers, takes you to the next level, and captures any audience no matter what the venue assuring a return gig and growing attention for your work as a musician. Listeners love to reflect and even reminisce when they hear a familiar song. On the same token you can "signaturize" your originals so that when your audience hears you, they can become familiar with what you are performing and look forward to it and maybe start requesting it.

Depending on where you live, you may find that covers are what most people want to hear especially if they are hearing you for the first time. Listeners will follow you wherever you perform and be opened to hearing your originals if your cover game is on point. The growing attention that you observe should encourage you that you are building a career that will continuously grow and keep you busy which is what you want. I would suggest that you pay attention to the trends as they happen so that you can stay in touch with your audience and strike while the iron is hot so to speak. So, let us delve deeper into the setlist creation concept:

As you are building a set list, if you google for instance "acoustic songs" or "acoustic covers to learn," you will see some of the same songs mentioned over again in every list. That is because there is something in those songs that captures the attention of the audience. So yes, you can strum your way through these songs, and they may be recognizable just by the progression and the vocals. In that case you will have people thinking to themselves " *wonder* if that's...." fill in the blank. What you want is "Wow I remember that song that was really well done!"

When you perform a song, you want 'ooohs' and 'ahhhs'. I know I do. So, in order to make it so that there will be no guessing as to what the song is play the signatures. People will go wild for that!

Most of these signatures are in the introduction. Take the time to learn that introduction. What I will do in this chapter is give you some examples of what you can do with the rhythm and the notes in the chords and quote some specific songs to demonstrate the musical points. What I would advise you to do is go the extra mile and don't take the easy way out on these songs that have important recognizable signatures.

3. Picking and Strumming

Making the strumming more intricate using some signature strum patterns. The audio will give you some great examples.

Ex. 27. "Good Riddance" (Time of Your Life)" by Green Day

Ex. 28. "Free Falling" by Tom Petty.

I will not do a full performance of these songs but will use the most recognizable chord and rhythm signatures to show you how to get them under your fingers.

4. Dynamics Matter

Much of the music that is out now is performed on one dynamic level. Loud! Dynamics or most basically understood as volume control are what make a song or instrumental piece great! Some songs start out loud with no head room (room for getting louder). A performer that uses a dynamic range is the one that gives you the goosebumps. You want to be that performer even if the song is not yours. Master the covers! So, this is about using your dynamics which is another way of saying taking command of your volume by crescendos (gradually increasing volume) and decrescendos (gradually reducing volume) as an expression of your dynamic control. I will demonstrate this through some samples on the CD:

Ex. 29. "Wish you Were Here" by Pink Floyd.

5. Let Your Fingers do the Talking.

Let us talk now about more intricate fingerstyle patterns. But before we do, a word on fingerstyle guitar. As a guitarist you will find if you do not know already that fingerpicking is an especially useful tool no matter what style of music interests you. It can offer a variety that will set you apart as a solo guitarist. If you haven't already, experiment with it and get some lessons on it and believe me a whole new world of performance capability will open up for you!

The examples I will use are:

Ex. 30. "Fire and Rain" by James Taylor (a timeless and popular piece) and

If you are not familiar with these songs look them up and give them a listen. In fact, look at *your* set list and re-familiarize yourself with those songs and see if you can work the signatures in whether they are rhythmic strumming or more intricate fingerstyle patterns.

Now I know that there are times on a gig that you just do not need to kill yourself by playing hard stuff, which is not what I am suggesting. I do say that for instance on a restaurant gig, listeners are listening more than you think. Never assume that you are not being heard. You may impress someone at that gig who will offer you a private party or another series of gigs throughout the prime of the season. Give them the signatures and have your promo material and CDs ready. Do not give up on selling your music!

Musically speaking using the same strum pattern for every song will limit your influence. Put the time in to change it up you will feel glad that you did!

Thomasina Winslow

 2019 EDDIES (Thomas Edison Music Awards) Blues Artist of the Year nominee, Thomasina Winslow is a singer and guitarist of top-level acoustic blues and more. Thomasina travels both nationally and internationally bringing the world of the blues to diverse audiences. Her performances are characterized by her snappy guitar chops and rich warm vocals.

Questions about the content of this book, purchase recordings, or to book performances and/or workshops you can contact Thomasina at:

Website: thomasinawinslow.com

Lesson inquiries: lessons.thomasinawinslow@gmail.com

Or write to:

Thomasina Winslow Music

P.O. Box 266

New Baltimore, NY 12124

© copyright 2021 Thomasina Winslow Music all rights reserved

www.ingramcontent.com/pod-product-compliance
Lightning Source LLC
Chambersburg PA
CBHW042333150426
43194CB00001B/50